D1567931

Submarines

By Kenny Allen

Gareth Stevens
Publishing

Please visit our website, www.garethstevens.com. For a free color catalog of all our high-quality books, call toll free 1-800-542-2595 or fax 1-877-542-2596.

Library of Congress Cataloging-in-Publication Data

Allen, Kenny, 1971-
Submarines / Kenny Allen.
    p. cm. — (Monster machines)
Includes index.
ISBN 978-1-4339-7180-8 (pbk.)
ISBN 978-1-4339-7181-5 (6-pack)
ISBN 978-1-4339-7179-2 (library binding)
1. Submarines (Ships)—Juvenile literature. I. Title.
VM365.A417 2012
623.825'7—dc23

                                            2011044223

First Edition

Published in 2013 by
Gareth Stevens Publishing
111 East 14th Street, Suite 349
New York, NY 10003

Copyright © 2013 Gareth Stevens Publishing

Designer: Daniel Hosek
Editor: Greg Roza

Photo credits: Cover, p. 1 Transtock/Masterfile.com; p. 5 Stephen Frink/The Image Bank/Getty Images; p. 7 Hemera/Thinkstock.com; p. 9 Steven Kaufman/Peter Arnold/Getty Images; p. 11 Sheldon Levis/ Photolibrary/Getty Images; pp. 13, 15 iStockphoto/Thinkstock.com; pp. 17, 19 U.S. Navy/Getty Images; p. 21 Time & Life Pictures/Getty Images.

Printed in the United States of America

CPSIA compliance information: Batch #CS12GS: For further information contact Gareth Stevens, New York, New York at 1-800-542-2595.

Contents

Sea Monsters! 4

Ship Shape 6

Time to Dive! 8

Inside Submarines 10

Engine Room 12

Speedy Sub 14

Jobs for a Submarine 16

The Ohio Class 18

It's a Typhoon! 20

Glossary 22

For More Information 23

Index 24

Boldface words appear in the glossary.

Sea Monsters!

A submarine, or sub, is a boat that can dive below the water. Some submarines are so small they can only carry a few people. Others are underwater monster machines. The largest submarines can carry more than 150 people!

Ship Shape

Submarines are long and smooth. They are narrower on each end. This shape allows them to move easily through water. A submarine's tower has a periscope. The periscope allows the crew to see above water when the submarine is below water.

tower

7

Time to Dive!

A submarine has tanks filled with air. They allow the sub to float like a regular boat. When the sub needs to dive, the tanks are filled with water. This makes the boat heavier. Some submarines can stay underwater for 6 months!

Inside Submarines

There's not a lot of room for people inside a sub. Crew members work for 6 hours then have 12 hours of free time. They sleep in small beds called bunks. Some officers have their own rooms, but they're small.

Engine Room

Submarine engines create power and electricity. Some subs have engines that burn **fuel**, somewhat like the engine in a car. Some have steam engines. Most military submarines today use **nuclear reactors**.

13

Speedy Sub

Submarines have giant propellers. Propellers have paddle-like parts that spin in the water to move the ship forward or backward. The fastest submarine ever built was the Russian K-222. It once reached 51 miles (82 km) per hour.

15

Jobs for a Submarine

Some submarines are used for undersea **exploration**. Some are used to repair **oil platforms**. Most are used by the military. Military submarines carry many **weapons**, such as **missiles**. Underwater missiles are called torpedoes.

17

The Ohio Class

The largest US submarines are those in the Ohio class, or type. There are 18 Ohio class subs. Each sub is 560 feet (171 m) long. The USS *Ohio*—the first of these subs—has been in use since 1981.

USS *Ohio*

19

It's a Typhoon!

Russian Typhoon class submarines are the largest ever built. They're 564.3 feet (172 m) long and can carry up to 160 crew members. They can stay underwater for up to 180 days and can dive 1,312 feet (400 m) underwater.

Typhoon Class Submarines

- **The first Typhoon class sub entered service in 1981 and is still in use.**

- **Only six Typhoon class subs were built. Work on a seventh began but was never finished.**

- **Each has two nuclear reactors.**

- **Each has two propellers.**

- **Each has its own swimming pool!**

Glossary

exploration: the act of traveling through an unfamiliar place to learn more about it

fuel: a source of energy for a machine

missile: a rocket used to hit something at a distance

nuclear reactor: a power plant that uses tiny pieces of matter called atoms to make energy

oil platform: an oil drilling rig at sea

weapon: something used to fight an enemy

For More Information

Books

Abramson, Andra Serlin. *Submarines Up Close*. New York, NY: Sterling, 2007.

Lock, Deborah. *Submarines and Submersibles*. New York, NY: DK Publishing, 2007.

Websites

How Submarines Work
science.howstuffworks.com/transport/engines-equipment/submarine.htm
Read more about submarines and how they work.

Submarine Force Museum
ussnautilus.org
Learn about submarines throughout history and "take a tour" of the first nuclear-powered submarine—the USS *Nautilus*.

Index

air 8

bunks 10

crew 6, 10, 20

dive 4, 8, 20

electricity 12

engines 12

exploration 16

fuel 12

military 12, 16

missiles 16

nuclear reactors 12, 21

officers 10

Ohio class 18

oil platforms 16

people 4, 10

periscope 6

power 12

propellers 14, 21

Russian K-222 14

shape 6

steam engines 12

swimming pool 21

tanks 8

torpedoes 16

tower 6, 7

Typhoon class 20, 21

USS *Ohio* 18, 19

weapons 16